T0005619

CACTUS QUEEN

Minerva Hoyt
Establishes Joshua Tree National Park

Written by
Lori
Alexander

Pictures by
Jenn
Ely

CALKINS CREEK
AN IMPRINT OF ASTRA BOOKS FOR YOUNG READERS
New York

"This desert... possessed me,
and I constantly wished that I might find
some way to preserve its natural beauty."
– Minerva Hoyt

Minerva tapped her foot and checked her watch. She was leaving Pasadena, California, with more than just her luggage.

Minerva traveled with prickly plants and twisted trees, stuffed jackrabbits, woodpeckers, and coyotes.

TAP...TAP...
TAP...

As a young girl, Minerva lived in Mississippi, far from the cacti and coyotes of the California desert. She loved outdoor adventures and long chats with friends.

In school, Minerva raised her hand high, never afraid to say what she thought. Words had power, and ideas could make a difference.

When Minerva grew up, she married Dr. Albert Hoyt. In 1897, they moved to Pasadena, California, near Los Angeles. Minerva didn't know a single person there. Could an outdoor adventure help?

Minerva hosted a party among the dazzling blooms of her sprawling garden. She enjoyed long chats with *new* friends.

BUZZZZZZ

SNIFF
SNIFF

When Minerva needed a break from the buzzing city, she took trips. First by horse and wagon. Later by automobile. Her favorite place was the Mojave Desert.

Wide and wondrous, it was unlike anything
Minerva had seen before.
Joshua trees dotted the desert in every direction.
Straight. Twisty. Short. Tall. These strange plants grew
nowhere else on Earth.

Minerva found herself visiting the desert more often,
especially after the death of her husband in 1918.
She nestled inside her sleeping bag atop the sandy
soil. The wind whistled through the Joshua trees.
Bright constellations swirled overhead.

hoooo hoooooooo wooooooo
hooo hoooooooooooo
wooooooooooo

"I stood and looked. Everything was peaceful, and it rested me."

In the 1920s, Los Angeles was a city on the go. There were more cars. More roads. More trips to the desert.

People loved the scenery so much, they wanted to keep some for themselves. Residents dug up Joshua trees, towering palms, fuzzy cholla, spiky yucca, and barrel cacti to keep in their backyards. Many of the desert plants didn't survive their move to city gardens.

BEEP!

BEEP!

BEEEEPP!!!!

Down went more Joshua trees.

Limbs and trunks were made into fences, corrals, and lightweight furniture—perfect for Hollywood stunts.

Nighttime motorists, lost on dark roads, set fire to the trees to find one another.

By the late 1920s, areas of the Mojave had been stripped almost bare. The desert plants never grew back. The desert animals lost their homes. Minerva wanted to help.

"This saving of the desert, if accomplished at all, must be done quickly, for there is already comparatively little left."

But not everyone cared about the desert. Not everyone cared what a woman had to say.

Many people thought the desert was a dry wasteland. A place they'd rather pass through than stop and admire.

If Minerva wanted to defend the desert, she would need to convince others that it was special. Even people who had never seen a desert before.

Minerva had a wild idea!

She would take a piece of the southwest . . . east!
She called on members of Los Angeles gardening
clubs. She called on artists, taxidermists, neighbors,
and friends.
    The desert was headed for New York City!

3770

The 1928 International Flower Show bustled inside a grand hall. Minerva arranged a desert display in a space the size of a classroom.

But something was missing. Minerva tapped her foot and checked her watch and waited. Delicate cactus blooms were unpacked just in time.

Curious guests couldn't stop talking about the strange landscape. Reporters took pictures. They called Minerva's exhibit *The Spirit of the Desert.* It won a gold medal.

The following spring, Minerva created displays in Boston and London. She won awards. More people were listening to her words. More people were loving the desert.

"No one who heard her talk could ever again regard the subject of conservation of desert flora with indifference."

—a fellow environmentalist

While removing plants from their natural environment was the exact thing Minerva was trying to stop, her mission was important. If she could get people to appreciate the desert, she could get them to protect the desert.

After the shows, she donated her displays to local museums. Interest in the desert bloomed. The first part of Minerva's plan had taken root.

In June 1933, Minerva was ready to pitch the next part of her plan. She wanted to save the desert by calling it a park. Not a small *state* park, but a well-known *national* park, 1,000,000 acres in size and protected by federal laws.

Minerva sat on the steps of the White House, patiently waiting to be seen by President Franklin D. Roosevelt. She brought two photo albums packed with images of the Mojave Desert.

She shared her photos. She shared her words:

"...we must see to it that parks are created in which the unique desert atmosphere and its matchless growth and its silence and mystery are preserved for the education and delight of the people."

After the meeting, a member of Roosevelt's team assured Minerva, *"The President is for this."*

All that remained was a land inspection from Roger W. Toll, superintendent of Yellowstone National Park in Wyoming. He would decide if Minerva's desert was worthy of national park status.

An icy March wind whipped around the inspector, and he shivered. After traveling along miles of dry land, he asked Minerva when they would arrive at her "park."

Where were the lush green trees, the roaring waterfalls, the crystal lakes?

Soon he filed his report: *"It is believed that the area is not suitable for a national park. It is not the outstanding desert area of the United States."*

The words prickled like cactus spines. But Minerva
didn't give up. Instead, she wrote letters. *Many* letters.
She persuaded others to do the same. Scientists,
teachers, politicians, and friends all put pens to paper:

Dear National Park Service . . .

. . . please send a
new inspector. . .

. . . someone who
**understands
California**. . .

. . . someone who
understands
the desert . . . .

For five months, letters flooded the National Park Service headquarters. A new inspection was scheduled—a second chance for the desert!

Assistant Director Harold C. Bryant lived in California. He knew all about desert plants and animals.

When he arrived for the tour, he was greeted by Minerva . . .

. . . and more than one hundred of her supporters.

Bryant inspected the land

from top

to bottom.

After three days, he agreed—Minerva's desert was worth saving . . .

Beautiful and brimming with life.

More About Minerva

Young Minerva

Minerva was born in 1866 in Durant, Mississippi, to a well-off family. Her father, Joel George Hamilton, was a state senator. Her mother, Emma Victoria Lockhart Hamilton, was a society matron. Minerva's parents taught her about politics and how to maneuver among the wealthy and the powerful. After marrying and moving to Pasadena, California, Minerva became involved in several organizations including the Los Angeles Symphony Orchestra, the Boys & Girls Club, the Red Cross, and the Valley Hunt Club, which founded the Tournament of Roses Parade.

After the death of her husband, Minerva put her social skills and influence to work. Her efforts at prestigious flower shows in New York, Boston, and London, and the creation of an International Deserts Conservation League, began to change people's attitudes about the desert. Inspired by her passion, Mexican president Pascual Ortiz Rubio set aside 10,000 acres of desert land as a monument. He nicknamed Minerva the "Apostle of the Cacti." But her struggle to protect desert landscapes in the United States would take many more years.

On August 10, 1936, President Roosevelt signed a law to create Joshua Tree National Monument, preserving 825,340 acres of desert land. It was slightly less than the one million acres Minerva was hoping for, as some of the land was already owned by railroad companies and the mining industry. Nearly fifty years after her death in 1945, the area gained even greater protection. In 1994, President Clinton signed the California Desert Protection Act, expanding the site and officially establishing Joshua Tree National Park.

Nearly three million people visit Joshua Tree each year. Once a year, the Joshua Tree National Park Association recognizes an individual or an organization that has been successful in studying, protecting, or preserving the desert. It's called the Minerva Hoyt Desert Conservation Award.

Because of its memorable appearance, the Joshua tree has become the symbol of the Mojave Desert. A Joshua tree:

- is not a tree *or* a cactus. It is the largest variety of the yucca plant.
- grows only in the Mojave Desert.
- typically reaches a height of 30 to 40 feet, though the tallest tree on record was 80 feet.
- lives for about 150 years, although some large specimens are thought to be much older.
- relies on one type of moth, the yucca moth, to pollinate it.
- may have inspired the Truffula tree in Dr. Seuss's *The Lorax*.

A desert tortoise gets most of its water by eating grasses and wildflowers.

Wildlife in Joshua Tree National Park

- While it may look deserted, the park is home to more than 400 types of mammals, reptiles, birds, insects, and amphibians.
- Many desert animals are active at night (*nocturnal*). These include coyotes, bobcats, deer, foxes, jackrabbits, snakes, bats, kangaroo rats, tarantulas, and scorpions.
- Birds, lizards, bighorn sheep, and desert tortoises may be easier to spot. They are more active during the day (*diurnal*).
- Desert animals have learned to adapt to their harsh, dry climate. Some can survive without water. They get the moisture they need from eating plants, seeds, and insects. Many burrow to escape the summer sun and winter chill.
- Desert plants also know how to adapt. Cacti have a waxy coating to keep cool and slow water loss. Most desert plants have a shallow root system, allowing them to take in as much water as possible during limited rainy seasons.

National Parks of the USA

- There are more than 400 areas protected by the National Park System, but only 63 have "national park" status. Additional areas include battlefields, monuments, reservations, and other historic sites.
- More than 300 million people visit national parks each year.
- Park features include caves, volcanoes, petrified trees, geysers, waterfalls, mountain peaks, lakeshores, or mile-deep canyons.
- Yellowstone was the first national park, established by President Ulysses S. Grant in 1872.
- Today, new national parks must be approved by both Congress and the president.

Joshua trees and wildflowers in spring

Author's Note

I grew up in San Diego, California, not too far from Joshua Tree National Park. Family camping trips to this special spot are some of my favorite childhood memories. By day, my brother and I scrambled up rock formations, racing for the best view of the Joshua tree forests. By night, we turned to star gazing and s'mores tasting. Many years later, I shared this same adventure with my own children.

In 2019, I read about a troubling incident at Joshua Tree. During a 35-day government shutdown, the park remained open with limited staff. It was impossible for the few on-duty rangers to monitor the park's 1,200 square miles. Visitors began to ignore the rules. They squabbled over campsites, scattered garbage, clogged toilets, and spray-painted boulders. They looped holiday lights around delicate Joshua branches. Other plants were cut down to make paths for racing off-road vehicles. This destruction took place over a handful of days, but experts estimate that it may take more than 200 years for the slow-growing Joshua trees to recover.

Minerva arranging her desert display at the 1928 International Flower Show in New York City.

Joshua trees outside park boundaries are not protected. Developers bulldoze to make way for more roads, houses, and shopping malls. In addition, drought and wildfires brought about by climate change affect the fragile desert ecosystem. Recent studies show Joshua trees are dying off in these hotter, drier conditions. Fewer seedlings are taking root to replace the older trees.

Learning about Minerva's mission was both inspiring and humbling. Her passion benefited not only the desert plants and animals but all of us who enjoy visiting this unique region. Vandalism, urban development, and the effects

of climate change prove the fight is not over. In 2020, a group of environmentalists raised their voices and wrote to the government—just like Minerva! They asked that Joshua trees be placed on the California Endangered Species list. The state agreed to temporarily protect all Joshua trees while a team further reviews the case.

Minerva used elaborate methods to bring attention to her cause, but simple changes can make a difference too. Check out the tips on the next page for some actions that may help protect the places *you* love best. —LA

Tips for Environmental Activists

1. Visit a national park and become a Junior Ranger. If you camp or hike, remove any litter and leave no trace of your stay.
2. Learn which plants are native and which are invasive in your area. Plant some natives in your garden or home and remove any invasives (make sure to properly destroy the plants so the seeds don't spread).
3. Use refillable water bottles and reusable food containers instead of single-use plastics.
4. Turn off the tap when brushing your teeth.
5. See how quickly you can shower or challenge yourself by taking a bath with very little water.
6. Carpool, ride your bike, walk or take a bus to school or your friends' houses.
7. Cook a meal with your family instead of going out to eat. Use fresh, locally grown foods, rather than packaged.
8. Donate your gently used clothes. Try shopping at thrift stores instead of buying new.
9. Turn off lights when not in use. Replace incandescent bulbs with energy-efficient LEDs.
10. To preserve night skies, use only outdoor lighting recommended by the International Dark-Sky Association.

THANK YOU, MINERVA!!

Selected Bibliography

All quotations used in the book can be found in the following sources marked with an asterisk (*).

"About Us." National Park Service. nps.gov/aboutus/index.htm.

Daley, Jason. "Joshua Trees Could Take 200 to 300 Years to Recover from Shutdown Damage." *Smithsonian* magazine, January 30, 2019. smithsonianmag.com.

*Dilsaver, Lary M. "Joshua Tree National Park: A History of Preserving the Desert." National Park Service History eLibrary. npshistory.com/publications/jotr/adhi.pdf.

Harris, Gloria G., and Hannah S. Cohen. *Women Trailblazers of California: Pioneers to the Present.* Charleston, SC: History Press, 2012.

*Hoyt, Minerva. "The International Deserts League." *Americana*, July 1931, 315–325.

*Kaufman, Polly Welts. *National Parks and the Woman's Voice: A History.* Albuquerque: University of New Mexico Press, 2006.

Martin, Brittany. "Experts Are Assessing the Damage Done to Joshua Tree During the Shutdown—and It's Grim." *Los Angeles Magazine*, January 28, 2019. lamag.com/citythinkblog/joshua-tree-goverment-shutdown/

"Minerva Hoyt." Joshua Tree National Park. nps.gov/jotr/learn/historyculture/mhoyt.htm.

Netburn, Deborah. "How a South Pasadena Matron Used Her Wits and Wealth to Create Joshua Tree National Park." *Los Angeles Times,* February 14, 2019. latimes.com/science/sciencenow/la-sci-col1-joshua-tree-minerva-hoyt-20190214-htmlstory.html.

"Reward Offered for Slayer of Giant of Desert," *South Pasadena Foothill Review*, June 27, 1930.

*Sorensen, Conner. "Apostle of the Cacti: The Society Matron as Environmental Activist." *Southern California Quarterly* 58, no. 3 (1976): 407–429.

Zarki, Joseph W. *Joshua Tree National Park.* Mount Pleasant, SC: Arcadia Publishing, 2015.

To my grandparents, Ken and Dolores, who loved road trips to the desert —*LA*

For my mother Jane, who like Minerva is a fierce force who inspires and alters the world around her for the better —*JE*

Acknowledgments

Thank you to the helpful staff at Joshua Tree National Park, from rangers to volunteers, who answered my in-person questions as well as my follow-up emails. Thanks to Alison Shoup, education specialist, who found the perfect reader for my manuscript. I'm grateful to Hannah Schwalbe, park ranger and public information officer, for reviewing the text and illustrations for accuracy. Also, a big thanks to Melanie Spoo, archivist and museum curator, who allowed me a peek inside the pages of Minerva's photo albums—the same ones viewed by President Roosevelt in 1933. And thanks to editor Carolyn Yoder and agent Kathleen Rushall, for their eagle-eyed edits and enthusiasm for this project.

Picture Credits

Minerva Hoyt family: 36 (top left), Daniel Elsbrock: 36 (bottom right), Hannah Schwalbe: 37;
Visual Studies Workshop / Contributor / Getty Images: 38.

Text copyright © 2024 by Lori Alexander
Illustrations copyright © 2024 by Jenn Ely
All rights reserved. Copying or digitizing this book for storage, display, or distribution in any other medium is strictly prohibited.

For information about permission to reproduce selections from this book, please contact permissions@astrapublishinghouse.com.

Calkins Creek
An imprint of Astra Books for Young Readers,
a division of Astra Publishing House
astrapublishinghouse.com

Printed in China

ISBN: 978-1-6626-8021-2 (hc)
ISBN: 978-1-6626-8022-9 (eBook)
Library of Congress Control Number: 2023905051

First edition
10 9 8 7 6 5 4 3 2 1

Design by Barbara Grzeslo
The text is set in Futura Std.
The illustrations are done in mostly acryla gouache,
with some smaller bits of colored pencil and collage.